LET EVERYONE FIND THEIR VOICE

Re-imagining the Psalms for Worship and Devotion

Lezley J. Stewart

SAINT ANDREW PRESS

First published in 2020 by
SAINT ANDREW PRESS
121 George Street
Edinburgh EH2 4YN

Copyright © Lezley J. Stewart

ISBN 978 0 71520 9844

All rights reserved. No part of this publication may be reproduced or transmitted in any form or by any means, electronic or mechanical, including photocopy, recording, or information storage and retrieval system, without permission in writing from the publisher. This book is sold subject to the condition that it shall not, by way of trade or otherwise, be lent, resold, hired out or otherwise circulated without the publisher's prior consent.

The opinions expressed in this book are those of the author and do not necessarily reflect those of the publisher.

The right of Lezley J. Stewart to be identified as author of this work has been asserted in accordance with the Copyright, Designs and Patents Act 1988.

British Library Cataloguing in Publication Data
A catalogue record for this book is available from the British Library.

It is the publisher's policy to only use papers that are natural and recyclable and that have been manufactured from timber grown in renewable, properly managed forests. All of the manufacturing processes of the papers are expected to conform to the environmental regulations of the country of origin.

Contents

	Introduction	v
	Notes on Using the Resources	ix
Refuge	Setting the Scene	3
	Psalm 91	4
	Psalm 46	6
	Psalm 62	9
	Suggestions for Liturgy	12
	Liturgy	13
Created	Setting the Scene	21
	Psalm 8	22
	Psalm 90	24
	Psalm 121	27
	Suggestions for Liturgy	29
	Liturgy	30
Lament	Setting the Scene	39
	Psalm 22	40
	Psalm 55	43
	Psalm 77	46
	Suggestions for Liturgy	49
	Liturgy	50

Centre	Setting the Scene	61
	Psalm 84	62
	Psalm 27	64
	Psalm 103	67
	Suggestions for Liturgy	70
	Liturgy	71
Pathway	Setting the Scene	81
	Psalm 23	82
	Psalm 1	84
	Psalm 16	86
	Suggestions for Liturgy	89
	Liturgy	91
Refreshment	Setting the Scene	99
	Psalm 63	100
	Psalm 145	102
	Psalm 42	105
	Suggestions for Liturgy	108
	Liturgy	110
Communion Liturgy		115
New Psalms	More than Words	125
	If Today	127
	Honest before God	129

Introduction

Much has been written about the Psalms and their use in the context of worship, both historical and contemporary. I cannot seek to do justice to such volumes in this introduction. Instead I will offer a brief insight into where these resources spring from, and my own approach to re-imagining the Psalms for worship today.

As a minister I have always been passionate about worship, the creation of contextually appropriate liturgies, and the intentionality of what we set out to do in worship. Creating the atmosphere and liturgical content that can cultivate a meaningful worship experience is a craft of sorts, and when it is done well it can lead to transformative encounters with God and with one another in faith.

Often in worship we are recalling ancient texts and applying them to give meaning in the present and the future. Essentially Scripture is the source of memory for many of our patterns of worship today. But how does Scripture speak of the wonder and mystery of God in a way that is relevant and contemporary?

For many people the Psalms provide this poetic invitation. The Psalms have always spoken to me as the *soul songs* of the Bible, while deeply framed in their own history. Yet in the Psalms we find a profound exploration of devotion to God in the midst of the heights and depths of all human experience that can offer a connecting point to those same experiences today. They have a timeless and universal connection, for though generations pass, the questions and experiences of humanity in relation to God remain the same.

I believe the Psalms invite us to wait upon God, but as ancient soul songs they also wait for new meaning to be applied to them by us from the context in which we find ourselves. This invitation is for all who participate in their sharing and allows the Psalms to lend themselves to the creation of new liturgical resources.

Liturgy is not just about the text but about culture and context. If devotion is to be encouraged as a mutual address between God and God's people, then liturgy must be in the hands of the people, and in a language that is shared. This essentially is my inspiration for what I describe as 're-imagining' the Psalms.

While the Psalms are often seen as the prayer book of the Bible, I wonder how they can break out of their historical context to become contemporary and living prayers. In many senses the Psalms arise out of an original question, and I seek to re-imagine them to address the questions as they might be expressed today.

My concept of re-imagining is based on a desire to facilitate the people of God in finding their voice in worship, through new expressions of ancient praise. Going beyond retranslating, I rather hope to capture something of the original emotion and immediacy of the Psalms to also inspire new Psalms. This is as a response to the call of Psalm 150 inviting all that has life and breath to praise God.

Understanding how the Psalter came to be shaped and formed over many years before finally being received in its current form into the canon of Scripture, provides a vibrant invitation to understand the Psalter's function as just the beginning of praise.

In many respects the concept of an *original* biblical Psalm is difficult to defend, as the evidence would suggest that the Psalms went through various stages of development and revision to reach the form we have today.

Understanding the Psalms primarily as devotional compositions is not to deny their history, formation or presumed intent, but sees the Psalter as a legitimate expression of the worship and wondering of God's people.

It is this authentic expression of emotion and experience in relationship to God that I believe can continue to inform our worship practices, encouraging the devotion of God.

The language of liturgy and prayer is always borrowed in some respects, but is transformed as people participate in what is expressed, allowing new things to be said as the words and expressions touch us and make an impact on our thinking and our emotions.

The Psalms specifically invite a partnership in prayer between God and the individual or community in their expression, and they often move from individual to corporate expressions. Many Psalms easily weave between the cry of an individual heart to a message of affirmation that is for the wider community. Taking that on board, these resources are offered both for individual prayer and devotion and for gathered worship.

My approach is one that allows for Scripture to speak outside its historical bounds, also embracing many things of which the Psalms speak – wonder, poetry, beauty and creativity. I believe Scripture finds its home in people of faith today who are asking questions, shared across the ages, in an embodied search for human understanding.

This approach to Scripture sees the Psalms as a means of encountering God. It is not the text that is to be revered but the God revealed within the text, in an active encounter of faith which can be transformative. Using a thematic and metaphorical approach, I have re-imagined a collection of Psalms within this framework.

One of the greatest challenges we face today is how people can experience God in a predominantly secular society. How can worship be authentically expressed and find its home in that sphere? How can worship remain a relevant expression of the questions, experiences and articulation of faith today, where old certainties are significantly changed or blurred, but people still seek to be able to express their faith?

I would suggest that the Psalms can continue to provide a powerful entry point, and allow us to keep talking to God with no particular boundaries or limitations.

Functioning as both words to God and words from God, the Psalms offer a rich resource for inspiring the devotion of God, where there is space for questions, lament, anger, hope, encouragement and praise, for people both as individuals and as part of a wider faith community. Using the Psalms
to embody these unchanging human experiences allows the Psalms to speak to us not only about God but about ourselves in relation to God. They reveal as much to us about ourselves and who we are, as we seek to understand our identity in God.

At the heart of this offering is the belief that the Psalms encourage the continuing praise of God and invite new expression. They offer a bridge for people to enter into the experience of worship where everyone can find their voice as a Psalmist. That at least is my prayer.

Notes on Using the Resources

The Psalms, which are re-imagined and arranged thematically, can be used as a springboard for contemplation in a variety of settings. They may lend themselves to meetings, small group worship, private devotion or public worship.

Each Psalm is followed by questions for consideration, and the reader/hearer is invited to respond from their own lives.

These Psalms can be used as the Scripture readings within the Liturgies that follow, or other readings can be chosen to suit. Some other readings and hymns are suggested for ease of use.

The Liturgies are written specifically for public worship, but can be used for private prayer and adapted by the user accordingly. Suggested responsive material is in bold print, but can be adapted or delivered by one voice.

The services offer space for reflective material or sermons.

The Confession can be shared and spoken aloud or offered for meditation in silence. The Conversation in Faith offers a space for an all-age talk or an opportunity to engage interactively with the theme, as best suits the context.

A Communion Liturgy is offered, which can connect to any of the Liturgies.

The New Psalms are offered for use in whatever contemplative setting is appropriate. My hope is that they act as an invitation for other new Psalms to come forth from those who use these resources.

May you find your own voice in the praise of God.

Refuge

Refuge
Setting the Scene

In today's world, refuge is a powerful and relevant theme for people in a variety of circumstances and settings. As in biblical times, when people were living with great uncertainty in life, today many uncertainties remain even if they are experienced differently.

Refuge offers and invites freedom. For the busy person this can be about space and the opportunity to breathe and be themselves. Refuge does not always suggest solitude, but can be found in activity and in the company of others.

Refuge can be a desire for peace and quiet and the absence of noise and disturbance. Such refuge is always in some sense fleeting, but can offer a sustaining pattern for life, and for prayer.

For others, it is about safety and hope of something better. Refuge can be the need to leave one's home and find a place to be and belong. Refuge can be found among family and friendships. For others it may be the need to escape from destructive relationships.

Refuge is not a distant concept from an ancient time, but continues to be shaped by how we experience and long for it today. God eternally speaks into this human search through the Scriptures and Psalms, and the theme lends itself to prayers and honest and open reflection.

Biblical expressions around the theme of refuge are full of emotion, and inviting contemplation around this theme may open up unexpected and surprising feelings. It is important to be able to accept and acknowledge this before God, holding onto hopeful expectation.

Psalm 91

Those who make their home in God,
who wrap themselves in the blanket of God,
can cling to a deeper peace.

The Faithful One provides warmth within;
sanctuary, from the fears that chill.

God secures the faltering spirit,
strengthening my resolve.
The voice that says,
'You can do this – I am with you.'

Those who hold onto God
have courage to face each challenge –
the darkness of the night,
the wounds of the day,
the waves that overwhelm.

A new day with God
announces again and again
a future and a hope.

God is faithful and near –
as close as our very skin.
No trouble is hidden;
no feeling is forbidden.

I will call upon the Eternal One.
My voice will be heard clear and loud:
'Answer me, in my need this day!'

God is the sanctuary of my life,
the one who hears my cry.

My hope lives again.

For Contemplation

Do I feel at home in God?

What are my fears and challenges this day?

What words from God echo in me?

Am I being honest with my feelings before God?

What hopeful vision can I hold onto?

Psalm 46

When the ground beneath you is shifting,
when you feel like you're losing your grip,
when you long for certainty and security –
know that God is still there.

Even when you fall down,
bringing blood to the skin
and tears to the eyes,
don't be afraid to pick yourself up
and begin again.

God's kingdom turns injury to promise –
a future where contentment can reign.
God has always been,
and will always be before you.

There is a healing balm
in the peace that God brings –
a tender touch to soothe and mend
the injuries of body and mind.

Chaos can lead to creativity
and new horizons appear ahead.
Those who were struggling are renewed
and carried forward with strength.

No matter what happens,
God is in this place.

The untrodden path offers a new adventure –
the discovery of what is yet to be.
God alone holds the answers,
but accompanies us in all our questions.

Be still,
know,
God,
present,
always.

For Contemplation

What is shifting for me at this time?

What brings me to tears?

What might contentment mean for me?

What new horizons are in my sight?

What questions am I living with?

Psalm 62

I breathe in the quietness,
enjoying the empty space,
trusting I am in the company
of the Holy One.
It is a good place to be.

Why do I let things wear me down,
making my spirit feel empty?
My thoughts hold strength
but are not reality.
God will not set me up to fail.

Why do people play power games?
What do they hope to achieve?
Nothing is gained in brokenness,
and no suffering should ever be silenced.

I breathe in the quietness,
enjoying the empty space,
knowing I am in the company
of the Holy One.
It is a good place to be.

My confidence finds its anchor;
my spirit feels renewed;
God is a safe haven for me.

Trust grows from this place –
to be honest and free in God.

Place and privilege are worthless –
they are delusions created by others.

Everything can change in an instant,
and life's gift is in the here and now.

Put no confidence in things that disappear,
but find blessing in the wisdom of the ages.
God has shared this story again and again,
and I will hold onto this truth.

For love is God's gift –
a place of security and sanctuary.

Find refuge there,
my friend,
and my soul.

For Contemplation

Where do I find the space to breathe?

What is draining my spirit?

Have I anchored myself in God?

What do I need to seize hold of today?

Am I living life with confidence and trust?

Suggestions for Liturgy

Creative focus

Use an image from a recent news story that speaks of refuge in some way.

Hymns

All my hope on God is founded
Dear Lord and Father of mankind
For everyone born, a place at the table
Give thanks with a grateful heart
God is our refuge and our strength
Lord, you have always been our home
Stay with me, remain here with me
When we are living, we are in the Lord

Scripture readings

1 Kings 19:4–10	Elijah seeking physical and spiritual refuge
Luke 6:12–16	After time with God, Jesus chooses the apostles
Isaiah 40:28–31	Confidence in the everlasting God
Mark 4:35–41	Jesus calms the storm

Ideas to develop

Why do we seek refuge in God? Does it serve only a personal purpose or does it lead to creative new beginnings and choices that are of much wider benefit?

When things are not within our own control, what does refuge in God mean, particularly when real dangers and fears are present? What does this mean in our complex world?

How can we help others discover the refuge that can sustain in the midst of every type of storm – mental, physical and spiritual?

Use personal stories that offer a variety of perspectives as to what refuge means. What does refuge mean if you are a refugee/homeless/isolated/exhausted?

Liturgy

Welcome

God invites us to worship as a community of faith. May you find the welcome of God here.
May our words frame a conversation with God.
Let everyone find their voice.

Invitation

Our help is in the Eternal; in God who welcomes us home.
Praise the One who is our safety, who sets us free to live.

(Psalm 124:6-8)

Prayer

Hear us, O God, in every prayer.
Lead us to your sanctuary and shelter.

(Psalm 61:1-3)

Our vision stretched, our eyes focused,
you invite us to see beyond the horizon.
With hearts opened, spirits raised,
you inspire us to wonder,
and call us to praise.

Great Comforter, you preserve all life;
in every waking moment you hold us close.
Though earth may sleep,
though eyes may close,
you are always active.
You move within us and without us,
welcoming us in this new day.

(Psalm 121)

Life of the world,
in your way, and in your truth,
we find you are always blessing.
May you find a home in our hearts,
so we might love and serve you.

Eternal Spirit,
take from us all strain and stress.
Let us find in our frailty
an openness and honesty before you.

Confession *(spoken or silent)*

**I need you, God – I seek your grace.
Into your open embrace
I place my fears and failings.
How long, O God, how long?**

**In forgiveness take from us
all that saps strength,
all that makes moan,
all that makes us question
how we might live again to praise you.**

(Psalm 6:1–6)

Comforting Words

God hears the simple prayers of the heart;
God has accepted our prayers this day.

(Psalm 6:9)

Response

You offer a sacred space – a place of welcome;
your love is our security and hope.
**Let everyone toast your goodness –
you are the Light of Life.
Amen.**

(Psalm 36:7–9)

Hymn

Conversation in Faith *(which may be concluded with the Lord's Prayer)*

Our Father in heaven,
hallowed be your name,
your kingdom come,
your will be done,
on earth as in heaven.
Give us today our daily bread.
Forgive us our sins
as we forgive those who sin against us.
Save us from the time of trial
and deliver us from evil.
For the kingdom, the power, and the glory are yours
now and for ever. Amen.

The Word of God *(readings from Scripture)*

Response to the Word

Open my eyes – inspire me to live and observe your word.
Open our eyes – let us understand the wonders of your ways.

(Psalm 119:17, 18)

This liturgy suggests the opportunity for three periods of reflection. You may wish to read a re-imagined Psalm then use its accompanying reflective questions, adding a further story or poem that relates to the theme. Alternatively use just one period for reflection, exploring a Psalm and its questions together, and adapt the order to suit. You can, of course, replace the reflections with a sermon and similarly adapt the order below.

Reflection/Sacred Space

Hymn

Reflection/Sacred Space

Hymn/Anthem/Music

Reflection/Sacred Space

Hymn

(If Communion is being celebrated, continue to page 117)

Prayer

We wait for you, O God *(silence)*

We rest in stillness
to know you as our security and strength.
A castle standing high on a hill,
you are our refuge.

We bring to you our worries and our wondering –
where is safety to be found?
How long will people be left outside?
When will peace be for all?

(Psalm 62:1–4)

In darkness, God, we call out to you.
Hear our prayer.

(Psalm 130:1–2)

We wait for you, O God *(silence)*

We bring to you our worries and our wondering –
when will the ways of the world be balanced and fair?
When will our hope not rest in wealth or power?
When will we realise what love can do?

(Psalm 62:5, 9–10)

**In darkness, God, we call out to you.
Hear our prayer.**

We wait for you, O God (*silence*)

Declaration

God has spoken.
Trust in God at all times – pour out your hearts freely.
God is a refuge for us. Amen.

(Psalm 62:5, 8)

Hymn

Blessing

Know that you have a home in God –
always, even now.
May God bless you
with this confidence and peace.
Amen.

For Reflection

What have I heard from God today?

What have I received?

How shall I live?

Let our worship continue in the unfolding of each day.
Let everyone find their voice.

Created

Created
Setting the Scene

Just as the Psalmist took inspiration from the beauty and cruelty of nature, the theme of creation offers us an invitation to contemplate on our interaction with everything that shapes our environment and world.

The metaphor of creation that springs from the Psalms encompasses the natural world around us and how we understand God and ourselves in relation to what we see, touch and experience, both around and within us.

Science has advanced our knowledge but also opened up many unanswered questions, and so the power of contemplating our place in creation, however that is understood, remains deeply meaningful.

We live each day making an impact on the places and people around us. We are also aware, in our increasingly connected world, of the forces of nature beyond our own small corner of the planet. In faith, we are called to recognise more widely our responsibilities as they affect all of God's creation.

The opportunity to share and shape our continuing questions and learning, and to do so in relationship with God and one another, can lead to new discoveries in how we understand our part in creation.

Psalm 8

God eternal,
in the tingling of the senses,
you are experienced all around.
You are praised in many ways.

Wonder abounds,
directing our thoughts to you.

We question nature and order,
the certainties of the past,
the discoveries of new days,
yet find you are not silenced.

You are in life and all we learn,
even if not known or fully understood.

How you care will always feed our questions –
why do we suffer pain and grief and loss?
How do we live and laugh and breathe?

We seek to know our place in your creation,
revealing something of your image.

Like the unfolding bloom,
offering colour and beauty,
we want to act with you,
so life may blossom for all.

God eternal,
in the tingling of the senses,
you are experienced all around.
You are praised in many ways.

For Contemplation

How do I sense God's presence?

What leads me to wonder?

What questions do I hold?

How can I reveal God's image?

How can I act with God in creation?

Psalm 90

From nothing you made us something –
you gave us a name, a place,
a home in you.
You are before and after time,
actively creating all things new.

We know our frailty before you.
We arrive and are gone
in the blink of an eye –
a shooting star in a galaxy of light.

Considering all that is transient,
help us make each day count.
You are always renewing and restoring,
and time and eternity are held in you.

You hold up a mirror before us
inviting us to see our reflection.
Our personal shadows sometimes overwhelm us,
but your light offers a fresh perspective.

In technicolour our lives play out before you.
Thousands of pixels join the good with the bad –
there is no hiding away,
for you are present in each unfolding scene.

Eternal One,
help us embrace the fullness of life
which is always your gift.
Viewed with your wisdom,
help us see the future pattern of our days.

Be patient with us,
as we are patient with you –
waiting, wondering, hoping,
and discovering our peace is in you.

Let sadness lead to celebration
and any pain find a partner in joy.
Your eternal love means
our home is always in you.

May our lives reflect your glory –
who you are and what you do.
Make us partners in your work,
creating, emerging, proclaiming –
our God makes all things new.

For Contemplation

What makes me aware of my own frailty?

What can I do to make this day count?

Do I see darkness or light in my own reflection?

Which scenes in my life do I need to own?

What am I waiting for and wondering about?

What can I do to proclaim God's goodness to me?

Psalm 121

I seek and search,
looking to people and places around,
asking ...
Who will help me?
Who will find me?
Who will make me whole?

Speaking freely, allowing the questions,
I hear an echo and an answer within –
that my help comes from God,
the creator and Eternal One.

God clears away the obstacles,
helping in unexpected ways.
For life is meant for fullness,
in the presence and peace of the Holy.

To know such protection,
around and within,
offers comfort in every strain
to body, spirit and mind.

For God will hold our life
secure in all creation.
God will keep us close,
living and thriving,
now and into the future.

Our help comes from God.
In God we are found.
In God we are whole.

For Contemplation

What am I searching for at this time?

What questions do I need to ask?

What does fullness of life mean for me?

How I do know when I am thriving?

Am I trusting in God's promised help?

Suggestions for Liturgy

Creative focus

Have a selection of stones available. These can be made into a cairn or used as a central focal point, or they can be selected/held or taken away.

Hymns

Before the world began, one word was there
Every new morning
For the beauty of the earth
Great is your faithfulness, O God my Father
Let all creation dance
My Jesus, my Saviour
O God, you search me and you know me
Sing to the Lord, with all of your heart
Today I awake and God is before me

Scripture readings

Genesis 1:26–7	Made in the image of God
Jeremiah 18:1–6	The potter's clay
Psalm 139	Fearfully and wonderfully made
2 Corinthians 5:16–21	A new creation in Christ

Ideas to develop

Explore what it means to be in the image of God. What image do we have of God and ourselves to begin with?

How do we understand God moulding and shaping our lives? What part do we take in this ourselves?

Use Psalm 139 as a meditative reflection with open-ended questions to explore.

How do we understand ourselves in relation to Christ and things being made new in Christ?

What examples of new life speak to us out of creation itself?

Liturgy

Welcome

God invites us to worship as a community of faith. May you find the welcome of God here.
May our words frame a conversation with God.
Let everyone find their voice.

Invitation

Let all creation praise you in wonder;
let your faithfulness be known.
**I will sing of your love and tell of your faithfulness.
Who can compare with you?**

(Psalm 89:1, 5–6)

Hymn

Call to Prayer

All that stretches beyond earth and sky inspires our wonder and praise.
Let us praise the Eternal, and rejoice in all that God is creating.

(Psalm 89:11–12)

Prayer

Creative God,
in the beauty of the world we sense you.
In rivers and rainbows,
sunlight and showers,
there is wonder that points beyond.
We sense your mystery
in colour and creativity.
Early morning hues paint the landscape;
night offers a muted palette of dreams.
You create new impressions every day.

We seek you in silence and serenity,
in turmoil and in storm.
We know that words cannot contain you,
and you speak in many ways.

We praise you for Christ,
who revealed beauty in love.
In humanity
he met with searching souls,
making wise the simple,
sharing in story and sign
your creative power.

We welcome the Spirit,
enlightening our minds,
inviting our questions,
challenging our fears,
helping us to explore further,
encouraging us to delve deeper.

We praise you in eternal mystery,
you are our heart's desire.

(Psalm 19:1–10)

(*Silence*)

Confession (*spoken or silent*)

**Before God,
and in the presence of God's people,
I search my heart.**

**Help me discern my faults;
protect me from proud thoughts.
Let the words of my mouth and the meditation of my heart
be acceptable to you.**

(Psalm 19:12–14)

Comforting Words

As wide as the wonder God inspires,
as deep as the searching God desires,
beyond all measure
is the forgiveness of God.

(Psalm 103:11)

Response

**I will give thanks to you, O God.
I will celebrate the reaches of your love and faithfulness. Amen.**

(Psalm 57:9–10)

Conversation in Faith *(which may be concluded with the Lord's Prayer)*

> **Our Father in heaven,
> hallowed be your name,
> your kingdom come,
> your will be done,
> on earth as in heaven.
> Give us today our daily bread.
> Forgive us our sins
> as we forgive those who sin against us.
> Save us from the time of trial
> and deliver us from evil.
> For the kingdom, the power, and the glory are yours
> now and for ever. Amen.**

Hymn

The Word of God *(readings from Scripture)*

Response to the Word

Listen to this teaching – hear what God has spoken.
Open our mouths and we will share these mysteries.

(Psalm 78:1–2)

Hymn/Anthem/Music

Prayer before Sermon
The word of God gives light, bringing understanding to all.
We turn to God, who keeps our thoughts.
(Psalm 119:129-30)

Sermon

Response after Sermon
We will not hide from the word and work of God.
We will tell of the wonders God has done.
(Psalm 78:4)

Affirmation (*standing*)
**We trust in the faithfulness of God, whose word lives in us.
We believe that God's love, revealed in Jesus Christ, is for all people.
In him we delight in life, and experience salvation.
We trust in the Spirit who stretches our vision.
We celebrate in God all that leads to greater understanding. Amen.**
(Psalm 119:89-96)

(*If Communion is being celebrated continue to page 117*)

Hymn

Prayer
With heart and voice we unite our prayers
in God, who is Maker and Mystery.

Eternal Creator,
you are the one who makes all things new.
You inspire hope for the earth and for all people.

When we look to the beauty of the earth,
the mountains that speak of time,
the lochs that fathom the deep,
we wonder at everything
cultivated with knowledge and wisdom.

We offer our thanks
for the wonder and mystery
of being one with you in Christ.
In him we see you always at work,
creating new harvests of hope.

We celebrate your Spirit's open reach,
calming the storms within our hearts.
You provide for our deepest needs,
sharing with us your way of life.

Knowing that in abundance there is also poverty,
we pray for all in barren landscapes –
where little thrives,
where resources are few,
where worry and fear reside.
We pray for all who are brought low,
who are trampled like weeds beneath our feet.

We pray for those who feel your absence,
who have become desensitised
to love freely given.
For all who live with abuse and violence,
we ask for your strength and freedom.

O God, who showers the earth with blessings,
we rejoice with those who celebrate,
we grieve with those who suffer.
We offer to you all that we are,
releasing the prayers of our hearts. (*Silence*)

God, you hear us and hold us.
Shape us more fully in your image,
that we might live and laugh,
hope and cry,
and come to love and serve
always in the way of Christ.

Declaration

God is always creating and renewing.
Those who trust the Eternal One cannot be shaken. Amen.

(Psalm 125:1-2)

Hymn

Blessing

You are created,
and are being recreated in God
each new day.
Live fully,
knowing this blessing,
of Creator, Sustainer and Friend.
Amen.

For Reflection

What have I heard from God today?

What have I received?

How shall I live?

Let our worship continue in the unfolding of each day.
Let everyone find their voice.

Lament
Setting the Scene

Lament is expressed fully and frequently in the Psalms. It is a release of the deepest and most profound emotion before God, without any boundaries. Nothing is off limits in this open exchange with God.

There is much we can learn and reclaim from the Psalms in their expressions of lament. Rather than expecting people to endure pain and turmoil in silence, the laments in the Psalms offer permission for us to be ourselves in the depths of every emotion that is experienced in the life of faith.

It is generally recognised that suppressing emotions is not healthy in the long term. In order to obtain health, healing and appropriate help, there is a need to be honest and real with what we feel in the midst of life. The same is true for anyone who has faith. The Christian faith does not make us immune to difficult experiences, nor does it ask us to be silent in facing such things.

The theme of lament explored in worship allows an honest articulation, shared in community, with the God who welcomes us. Everything does not need to be joyful in the presence of God, and it is good to acknowledge that fully.

Opening up the opportunity to lament may release some otherwise hidden feelings and emotions. A worship leader should be pastorally sensitive to how people might respond.

The exploration of this particular theme may lend itself especially to reflective worship, with plenty of opportunity for space. The linking with the Communion service may also be both helpful and healing.

Psalm 22

Exhausted and feeling alone,
I cry out in my pain.
No one is listening –
I am nothing.

Others say they find comfort in God
but I just feel empty –
I am treated as worthless.
Does anyone really care?

I hear an inner voice whispering,
'God created everything with value.'
Come close then, God;
help me believe this is true.
Take me out of my thoughts
so I can find myself in you.

Weary and worn out,
I'm just a shadow of myself.
Life's stresses and strains
have sapped my energy.
Come close now, God,
and give me your strength.

There's a bubbling up within me –
some new source of energy.
I surprise myself with a smile,
and those around me notice it too.

I know it is you.
I name it is you –
God gives me hope again.

As I find my freedom from fear
your promise is for all to see.
You offer me choice and change
and I will walk forward with you.

I will add my voice to your story.
Your love and faithfulness will be remembered.
For you give life its purpose
and let me begin again with hope.

I honour you by living my life,
beginning today,
and trusting in tomorrow,
showing what God can do.

For Contemplation

Am I taking time to listen to my own thoughts?

Am I able to be honest with others?

What needs to change?

How can that change begin?

Am I embracing freedom from fear?

What step forward will I take?

Psalm 55

I find myself distraught
and trouble swells within me.
My stomach churns, my head pulses –
I can't find release.

I need someone to help me –
I can't cope with this alone.

Come close, I pray.
Hold me and hear me.
My whole being is hurting
and I feel overwhelmed.

I wish I could escape somewhere –
away from all I feel;
to be able to get through this
and come out safe on the other side.

I am shaken by my experiences.
To be hurt by those you trust
runs deep, like a wound,
leading to questions and self-doubt.

When what was certain is gone,
and joy is all but lost,
anger becomes a friend –
though I fight its grip on me.

I call on you, God, to help me.
You are stronger
than any destructive thoughts.
I cast my burdens on you.

As I learn what only I can control,
your faithfulness becomes my strength.
Hard as it may be,
you ask me to trust you with the rest.

Your wisdom is my guide –
I begin to heal as I let go.

I am loved and held by you,
my companion, my friend:
God, in whom I trust.

For Contemplation

What is at the heart of what I feel?

Who might share my burden?

Have I wounds that need help to heal?

Have I let anger become my friend?

Have my thoughts become greater than reality?

What wisdom will I let be my guide?

Psalm 77

In the darkness of night
my emotions are set free.
The pain I feel pulses within me
as I confront my deepest fears.

I have little energy to summon,
and nothing calms my mind.
Absence overwhelms me
and I wonder, where is God?

I try to recall when things were different,
when I didn't feel this way.
In the recesses of my mind
I search, with hope, to remember.

I am consumed by this present darkness –
it occupies my heart, my body, my mind.
It makes me question everything;
where is God to be found?

As I name my pain and fear,
I wonder if I've become stuck.
Do I find it easier to stay in darkness
than risk moving into the light?

There are memories that spark my senses,
reminding me of better days.
When I felt God's presence with me,
I knew purpose and comfort in life.

You have done wonders for me, O God,
and I believe you will again.

You are always faithful –
I will trust I am in your hands.

In this vortex of emotions
I look for the eye of the storm.
I will find your presence and peace,
though trouble may remain.

You invite me into your light
and offer a way to move forward.
Let me take this step with courage,
trusting you will guide me through.

For Contemplation

What is my dominant emotion at this time?

What questions do I want to ask before God?

Am I being honest with myself?

Have I become stuck in my thinking?

Am I trusting in God's faithfulness?

Will I respond to God's invitation?

Suggestions for Liturgy

Creative focus

Using candles might be helpful, and providing the opportunity to light or extinguish, depending on feelings of hope (light) and despair (extinguish).

Hymns

Beauty for brokenness
Comfort, comfort now my people
Even though the rain hides the stars
I waited patiently for God, for God to hear my prayer
Inspired by love and anger
O God, you are my God alone, whom eagerly I seek
Up from the depths I cry to God
We lay our broken world in sorrow at your feet
We turn to God when we are sorely pressed

Scripture readings

Matthew 23:37–9	Jesus laments over Jerusalem
John 11:28–37	Sadness at the death of Lazarus
Job 3	Job's lament
Psalm 43	Praying in a time of trouble

Ideas to develop

How might the example of Jesus be used to help in the expressing of our feelings and emotions in relationship to God?

Explore anger, particularly in situations of bereavement and loss, and how Scripture gives example and permission for this.

What would our own lament be? Might it be a helpful tool to explore?

How do we shape and create opportunities for prayer that allow for lament?

Liturgy

Welcome

God invites us to worship as a community of faith. May you find the welcome of God here.
May our words frame a conversation with God.
Let everyone find their voice.

Invitation

Come as you are – heavy heart and troubled minds are no barrier to God.
All time is in God's hands – in this I trust.
Let life and love shine through.

(Psalm 31:9, 10, 14–16)

Hymn

Call to Prayer

Listen to my prayer and hear my cry.
Surround me with your peace and presence.

(Psalm 61:1, 4)

Prayer

There is an eternal welcome,
a whisper that echoes
and repeats again –
come close to God and be at peace,
beyond all understanding.

Eternal One, we seek your peace,
at this time,
in this place,
and in each testing moment.

While light has its origin in you,
we sometimes hold only the darkness.
Help us draw close and sense
what we cannot always see.

In silence, our souls wait for you.

(*Silence*)

Teach us that emptiness waits to be filled,
that doubt isn't something to fear,
and despair can give birth to hope.
All things are held together in you.

Help us to trust you,
even when we have no faith in ourselves
or in the goodness of others.

In silence, our souls wait for you.

(*Silence*)

Through Christ,
remind us that the lost can be found,
the broken can be healed,
and new life is always beginning.

Keep faith with us we pray,
even when our own faith is faltering.

Confession (*spoken or silent*)

Turn to me, O God, and be kind.
In every absence, be a presence.
My heart is heavy
and troubles weigh me down.
Consider my faults and be forgiving,
that I may find relief and rest in you.

(Psalm 25:16–18)

Comforting Words

God's faithfulness can never end –
it is established from the beginning to the end of time.
It is an unbroken promise for you,
and for all people, everywhere.

(Psalm 89:1–2)

Response

I will claim your promise and your peace.
I will find your calm in the storm. Amen.

(Psalm 89:8–9)

Conversation in Faith (*which may be concluded with the Lord's Prayer*)

> Our Father in heaven,
> hallowed be your name,
> your kingdom come,
> your will be done,
> on earth as in heaven.
> Give us today our daily bread.
> Forgive us our sins
> as we forgive those who sin against us.
> Save us from the time of trial
> and deliver us from evil.
> For the kingdom, the power, and the glory are yours
> now and for ever. Amen.

Hymn

The Word of God (*readings from Scripture*)

Response to the Word

Give thanks for the gifts of God.
Open my heart and my soul to receive.

(Psalm 108:1)

Hymn/Anthem/Music

Prayer before Sermon

Speak to us, God, in our time of need.
Our help comes from you.

(Psalm 108:12)

Sermon

Response after Sermon

The promise of God stands for all generations.
We are called to tell the story.

(Psalm 103:17)

Affirmation (*standing*)

**We trust in the one who hears the honest expressions of the heart –
in the God who gave us voice and hears our cry.
We celebrate the invitation to be in the company of the Holy,
in good times and in bad.
We commit ourselves to living in God's presence and peace,
finding rest for our souls,
and giving thanks for the gifts in each new day.**

(Psalm 116:1-7)

(If Communion is being celebrated, continue to page 117)

Hymn

Prayer

You have been here before us,
and you will remain after us.
The prayers we bring
are not brought in our hearts alone,
but they are shared
in your love and wisdom.

We ask you to heal and help;
to direct and guide the future yet to be
for those people and situations
we name before you now.

(Silence)

We pray for those
who are feeling weary and lost this day,
that they might have renewed strength
for whatever steps lie ahead.
With your help, O God,
may each day bring new resolve.

We pray for those
who need patience at this time,
when progress and treatment is slow,
and the future is hard to contemplate.
For all in pain and discomfort,
we pray for your healing touch.

We pray for courage,
for those who need it most.
When disappointment obscures the way of hope,
and every pathway seems full of obstacles,
may you lead the way unknown.

We pray for wisdom,
that those who have trusted in your promises
might know them to be real and true.
Reassure us all, we pray,
that your presence is for now and always,
and by our side you will stay.

We pray for all who doubt;
finding it hard to believe in your goodness.
We ask that in your mystery
you would draw close.
May your love and presence
be found in the care and compassion
of another – even us.

We pray for your world,
where there is much hurt and need –
with much pain and injustice,
and not enough hope.
We pray that we might help your kingdom come,
being your partners in prayer and action.

Declaration

God keeps faith for ever.
I will find hope and happiness with God. Amen.

(Psalm 146:5-6)

Hymn

Blessing

God receives all that you release.
Trust in that blessing.
God is comfort, strength and hope,
for you, and all in need.
Always.
Amen.

For Reflection

What have I heard from God today?

What have I received?

How shall I live?

Let our worship continue in the unfolding of each day.
Let everyone find their voice.

Centre

Centre
Setting the Scene

Centre, as one of the themes of this book, is not explicitly from the biblical Psalms. Instead it is intended to encompass something of the contemporary understanding of that which roots and centres us as human beings, and people of faith.

In this exploration of the Psalms, and re-imagining their expression, this theme invites us to think about how we understand God at the centre of things. It can allow for contemplation of both the inner life and the way we live in community, as we seek to understand ourselves more fully in relation to God.

In recent years, a prevalence of words have been added to our vocabulary that have a 'self' prefix, such as self-examine or self-determine. Rather than understand this as a 'self-seeking' movement, it perhaps suggests that our own identity is key and is essentially tied up with how we experience most things in life and faith.

The invitation to contemplate what is at the centre gives an opportunity in worship to explore priorities and boundaries, and consider everything that resources individual life and faith in Christ.

To have a sense of self is important in instilling confidence and faith in all that God inspires in each of us. Community is shaped and formed from the bringing together of our lives, connected by God.

Psalm 84

O God, you are my centre.
I seek you in the unfolding of each day.

For this I long –
to be where the Spirit is living
and know my place is there.

Doesn't everyone seek such a space?
A place to thrive and be.
Happy are those who find this gift.

With you as the centre
life stretches out
gently, generously,
touching, connecting, sharing –
creating a rippling effect.
You inspire moments of praise,
securing hope and strength deep within.

Centre and source, you are not hidden.
You are living and breathing,
crafting and composing the pages of the story
where I am named and known.

O God, you are the centre.
Happy are those who dwell in you.

For Contemplation

Where is God to be found today?

Am I in a thriving place?

What ripples can I detect in this community, connecting God, myself and others?

What words of praise rise in me?

Is God at the centre of my life?

Psalm 27

Why do I worry when I know you are there?
Why do I let things overwhelm me?
As I repeat to myself, like a mantra,
'God is light and life',
I find again my centre
and rest in the Holy One.

Like the cork set free from a bottle,
the pressures I hold find release.
You are close in every experience –
my calm and my confidence.

I will always seek reassurance –
you made me human, after all!
My daily challenge
is to trust and believe
that my heart beats in time with yours.

For you give me life and love,
offering space and inner peace.
My spirits soar from this source –
I smile, I sing, I am moved to praise.

When my confidence falters,
hear me and help me.
Challenge my fear when,
quickening and pulsing,
I feel only my own heart beating.
Restore a right rhythm within me.

Inspire me for each new challenge,
knowing that you are part of the adventure.

Don't let me imagine the hurdles ahead,
but help me look for the opportunities.

Trusting and believing,
centring my soul in you,
I wait with anticipation
to embrace new horizons.

With you,
I have the courage
to see all things through.

For Contemplation

What is it I am worrying about?

What do I need to hear to regain my centre?

Am I remembering that it's OK to seek reassurance from God?

What knocks my confidence?

What opportunities can I see ahead?

How shall I keep strong?

Psalm 103

With my whole being
I give thanks to God.

I praise the Holy One,
the source of my joy.
I celebrate each gift,
and all good things in life.

Rooted in God,
life finds a new focus
and energy flows within.

These things I know –
God loves and forgives,
heals and restores.

The One who welcomed me in
is my life's inspiration.

I turn to God
to centre myself each day –
to set aside all that is destructive,
and live with love and grace.

There is no end to God's goodness;
the only limit is my imagination.
Such love is beyond compare
and I thrive in this gift.

Some things are so transient,
changing on a whim.
But life in God is eternal,
to be celebrated again and again.

God is near – now and always,
the centre and source of all.
Hope – believe – trust –
in God you will live fully.

Give thanks to God,
with heart,
with soul,
with voice.

For Contemplation

What am I able to celebrate today?

What is God asking me to focus on at this time?

How does my life speak of God's inspiration?

Is there anything I need to set aside that is destructive?

Am I embracing the fullness of life God offers?

What can I give thanks for in this moment?

Suggestions for Liturgy

Creative focus

If possible use a circular worship set-up, so that the central focus is on being gathered together in community.

Hymns

All I once held dear, built my life upon
As we are gathered, Jesus is here
Be still for the presence of the Lord
Christ be beside me
Come and find the quiet centre
Focus my eyes on you, O God
Lord, I lift your name on high
Take, oh take me as I am

Scripture readings

Luke 19:1–10	Zacchaeus chooses a new path
Mark 5:25–34	Jesus heals
Luke 21:1–4	The widow's offering
Ephesians 4:1–6	Unity in Christ

Ideas to develop

What does it take to help us refocus and seek a new direction or path? Do we need to be challenged and hear the questions God might be asking us?

Jesus heals a woman in the centre of another healing story. Do we always notice where our focus lies, and what lies beyond?

Sometimes priorities and sacrifices are made obvious. Sometimes they mean we have to choose. How do we shape our priorities as Christians with God at the centre?

What is it that unites us in all the diversity we know and celebrate in life? Can we learn from the words of Paul in Ephesians about what centres us and creates community together?

Liturgy

Welcome

God invites us to worship as a community of faith. May you find the welcome of God here.
May our words frame a conversation with God.
Let everyone find their voice.

Invitation

Come and wonder at the Eternal; let everyone stand in awe.
God spoke, and it came to be – God commanded, and it stood firm.

Happy are those who seek after God – the people who accept this invitation,
those who wait on God and place their hope in love.

(Psalm 33:8, 9, 12, 18)

Hymn

Call to Prayer

I call upon you, O God. Listen to my voice when I call to you.
Let my prayer be an offering to you. My heart and voice are yours.

(Psalm 141:1–2)

Prayer

Eternal One,
there is no ending and beginning with you.
You are before and behind
and dwell in mystery within all things.
You are always at the centre,
inviting us in to meet with you.

All that has beauty flows from you.
We wonder at everything within and around us,
the majesty of what you have revealed,
and are revealing still.

We praise you for coming close in Jesus Christ –
one with you, and one with us,
shedding light and truth
in his words and ways.
His voice echoes in the living of all our days,
calling gently, yet powerfully,
'Follow me.'

Gentle and vibrant Spirit,
you stir our imagination
and stretch our vision.
You call us to continue with passion
Christ's witness in the world.
Strengthen us
and resource us from within,
that we might carry this gift –
the message of life in fullness for all.

Source of all goodness,
you call us to live in your freedom.
You know what brings us low,
and the deep and dark silences
that make for heavy hearts.
You offer to the body and spirit
what we need now,
and what we need for life to come.

You call us to find a place of safety in you,
where nothing need be hidden.
You hear us and you hold us,

offering release and refreshment.
We gladly approach at your invitation.

(Silence)

Confession *(spoken or silent)*

Forgive me, O God.

**In the strength of your love,
wipe away all that is wrong –
let me be made new.**

**Trusting in your deep wisdom,
refresh my heart, O God.**

**From a place of honest reflection,
let me find the words to praise you.**

**Surround us with your Spirit.
Let there be no distance between us,
that we might delight in you.**

(Psalm 51:1-3, 10-12, 15-17)

Comforting Words

Much further than the reach of sight or sound is the love of God.
God's loving embrace is our forgiveness.

(Psalm 103:11, 12)

Response

**I will celebrate that you have lifted me up –
you have set me free.
I called out to you, and you heard me and helped me –
your healing brings me life.
Let us bless God's name together,
for your anger is fleeting
but your faithfulness is for ever.
Thanks be to God. Amen.**

(Psalm 30:1-5, 12)

Conversation in Faith *(which may be concluded with the Lord's Prayer)*

> Our Father in heaven,
> hallowed be your name,
> your kingdom come,
> your will be done,
> on earth as in heaven.
> Give us today our daily bread.
> Forgive us our sins
> as we forgive those who sin against us.
> Save us from the time of trial
> and deliver us from evil.
> For the kingdom, the power, and the glory are yours
> now and for ever. Amen.

Hymn

The Word of God *(readings from Scripture)*

Response to the Word

Teach me, O God, the way of your wisdom and I will observe it to the end.
Give me understanding, that I may embrace your word with my whole heart.

(Psalm 119:33, 34)

Hymn/Anthem/Music

Prayer before Sermon

Show us your steadfast love, O God,
and give us your salvation.
**Let me hear what God will speak
to all who turn their hearts to God.**

(Psalm 85:7, 8)

Sermon

Response after Sermon
Your word, O God, is truth.
Let it live in me for ever. (Psalm 119:160)

Affirmation
We declare to you what was from the beginning:
what we have heard, what we have seen with our eyes,
what we have looked at and touched with our hands, concerning the word of life –
this life was revealed, and we have seen it and testify to it,
and declare the eternal life that was with the Father and was revealed to us –
we declare what we have seen and heard so that you also may have fellowship with us;
and truly our fellowship is with the Father and with his Son Jesus Christ.
We declare these things so that our joy may be complete.
This is the message we have heard from him and proclaim to you –
that God is light and in him there is no darkness at all.
(1 John 1:1–5)

(If Communion is being celebrated continue to page 117)

Hymn

Prayer
With one heart and voice we give thanks to God.
We bring an offering of praise for every gift and blessing,
presenting ourselves to God
who is the searcher of all our hearts.

We worship the One who has shaped our being,
who has set our course –

offering in mystery and majesty
the way of truth and life.

Your love sustains us and centres us,
freeing us to pray for one another –
everything is held together in you.

Source of all, you carry our trouble and pain;
you take to your heart our grief and worry –
you want to make your people whole.

May the words of my lips rise to you;
may our thoughts deep within find release;
may the Spirit give life to all people;
O God, our source, and our strength.

(Psalm 19:14)

In the sanctuary of silence,
we excavate our memories, thoughts and questions.
Delving deeply,
we release our hopes and concerns,
to one another and to you, O God.

May the words of my lips rise to you,
may our thoughts deep within find release;
may the Spirit give life to all people;
O God, our source, and our strength.

We pray for situations of concern *(silence or words)*
(in our world, in our community, in our church, in our circle of family and friends)

May the words of my lips rise to you,
may our thoughts deep within find release;
may the Spirit give life to all people,
O God our source, and our strength.

Loving Christ,
you have transformed life and death,
bringing hope and light.
Assure us that those who rest in your company
know the peace of eternity,
and unite us with all in earth and heaven.

Declaration

You are my God, and I will give thanks to you.
You are my God, and I will praise you.
O give thanks to God, for every goodness.
God's love endures for ever. Amen (Psalm 118:28, 29)

Hymn

Blessing

The blessing of the God of life,
the blessing of the Christ of love,
the blessing of the Spirit of peace,
centre and sustain you,
now and for evermore.
Amen.

For Reflection

What have I heard from God today?

What have I received?

How shall I live?

Let our worship continue in the unfolding of each day.
Let everyone find their voice.

Pathway

Setting the Scene

Pathway as a theme immediately suggests a journey and lends itself to the exploration of all the twists, turns and different directions in the life of faith.

Pathway is a repeating metaphor in the Psalms and translates with ease into how we encounter the adventure of faith today, albeit in a different landscape from that known by the Psalmist.

There is much to explore from a variety of approaches in worship, which can be as varied as the pathways that people are on!

Some are searching for a pathway that leads closer to God. Others have taken a turn away from God but may be struggling to engage honestly about this. Some may be seeking release from a destructive pathway, or one that has simply led to disappointment and pain.

In the context of worship this theme invites an encounter that understands that God is in company with us, in every experience, yet acknowledging that we can often feel as if we walk alone.

The challenge is to try to express, beyond the beauty of the ancient poetry found in the Psalms, words that connect with the journeys that are being experienced in the here and now.

By seeking to connect with the thoughts and feelings of those who are exploring new pathways, we may be able to open up to new opportunities and expressions of that continuing adventure with God.

Psalm 23

God is a pathway for my life.
I find peace when I am with God.

Even on rough ground,
even in darkness,
even when the direction is unclear,
God is with me.
I am never alone.

Way-markers guide my steps,
offering pointers to my next turn.
Christ walked this path before me –
he is my companion on the road.

Step by step,
this pilgrim path sustains me.
Step by step,
freedom in Christ is found.

The Eternal One secures my life,
leading me always forward.

I will praise God while I live and move.

For Contemplation

Which pathway am I following?

What is the lie of the land?

How do I allow God to direct me?

Have I missed a turn?

Have I found peace and freedom in Christ?

Psalm 1

When you find the good path
and know you don't hold all the answers,
you begin to arrive.

When you are not easily distracted,
but own and name what grounds you,
you are becoming secure.

When you discover contentment
in all that feeds you –
body, mind and spirit –
you are in the company of
the Holy One,
who was always there.

This is a sustaining place –
being alive to God's presence.
Twists and turns hold no fear,
but offer adventure and learning.

God's invitation is always open,
and barriers are our own creation.
There is no enjoyment in being lost,
or seeing others fail.

Lead us all in the path of peace,
where life is full,
and people flourish.

Happiness is God's gift,
waiting to be found.

For Contemplation

Do I feel that I'm on a good path?

How do I recognise my distractions?

What is feeding me each day?

Am I open to God's invitation?

What is my definition of happiness?

Psalm 16

In your presence, God,
I discover a deep peace.
My feet find a firm path,
securing my life's direction.

Others have travelled this way,
inspiring new disciples.
Let me take simple steps,
revealing your way by example.

Some paths lead to sadness –
even those we don't really choose.
Help me not get lost or distracted,
but walk always in step with you.

I love you, my God,
and I choose your way.
This is your path,
and I know my place is here.
Your guidance is life's gift,
to navigate each adventure.

I'm not a puppet on a string –
the decisions and choices are mine.
You offer me the wisdom of the ages,
opening every direction before me.

I choose to follow you,
and find security in each step.
Contentment is a welcome friend,
with you as my companion.

I trust in your faithfulness
and seek to follow faithfully.
I celebrate your way –
the challenge and the opportunity.

With you, O God,
is life and joy;
happiness,
and peace of mind.

Your path offers new direction –
I will embrace this
today, tomorrow,
and for evermore.

For Contemplation

What is filling me with peace today?

How am I living by example?

Is there anything distracting me from God's path?

Do I feel secure in my choices?

Am I excited by the opportunities before me?

Do I feel secure in God's company?

Suggestions for Liturgy

Creative focus

It may be helpful to ask people to doodle their own journey of faith, noting key people, encounters and obstacles along the way.

Hymns

Brother, sister, let me serve you
From the falter of breath
I will offer up my life in spirit and truth
Look forward in faith
Lord, for the years
Praise, I will praise you, Lord, with all my heart
Seek ye first the kingdom of God
Will you come and follow me?

Scripture readings

Exodus 3:7–12	Moses is called to lead the Israelites
Philippians 3:12–21	Pressing on further
Luke 24:13–35	The road to Emmaus
Proverbs 3:1–8	Choosing the right path

Ideas to develop

How can we inspire one another to respond to new directions from God, when things feel impossible? How does this relate to challenges to the Church at this time?

Do we take enough time to consider our faith journey with the expectation of going further? Where have we come from, where are we now, and what are we pressing towards?

Explore through personal stories how we encounter God in the stranger and have our eyes opened. What do we learn from such journeys, and what might we miss if we close our minds along the way?

Allow the reading from Proverbs 3 to invite reflection on stages along the way – personally and in community together. Use each verse to reflect on the path God might be preparing at this time.

Liturgy

Welcome

God invites us to worship as a community of faith. May you find the welcome of God here.
May our words frame a conversation with God.
Let everyone find their voice.

Invitation

God is near to all who search for truth.
God hears each cry and knows each need.
I will call on the One who holds all life.
I will praise the One who guides me.

(Psalm 145:18-21)

Hymn

Call to Prayer

Seek God with all your heart. Let your heart be open.
You have always heard my cries.
You have always been there before me.

(Psalm 27:7-8)

Prayer

We turn to the One who is named and known,
who has been faithful in every generation.

In this community of faith,
and with those who have walked before us,
we worship the God who calls us here.

Following in the footsteps of faith,
standing in the footprints of Christ,

we respond to God
who is love and mystery –
the One who leads us,
teaches and inspires us,
day by day.

We call to mind the goodness of God,
who sustains our life with hope.
In Christ we discover the way,
the truth and life,
and find that he walks with us.

In stillness now we offer
our thanksgiving and praise
to the One who has gifted us life
and shown us the path to follow.

(*Silence*)

Confession (*spoken or silent*)

God, though I try to stay on your path
I often take the wrong turn.
Test my sense of direction,
show me where I lose the way,
and bring me back on course
through your love and faithfulness. (Psalm 26:1-3)

Comforting Words

God retrieves you and redirects you –
walk forward with integrity. (Psalm 26:11)

Response

My feet stand again on level ground.
I return to God, my guide. Amen. (Psalm 26:12)

Conversation in Faith (which may be concluded with the Lord's Prayer)

Our Father in heaven,
hallowed be your name,
your kingdom come,
your will be done,
on earth as in heaven.
Give us today our daily bread.
Forgive us our sins
as we forgive those who sin against us.
Save us from the time of trial
and deliver us from evil.
For the kingdom, the power, and the glory are yours
now and for ever. Amen.

Hymn

The Word of God (readings from Scripture)

Response to the Word

Happy are those who walk in the way of God.
They grow and prosper in all they do.
**I will delight in your word,
and walk in your ways.**

(Psalm 1:1–3)

Hymn/Anthem/Music

Prayer before Sermon

**Your word is a lamp to show us the way.
Your word brings light to our steps.**

(Psalm 119:105)

Sermon

Response after Sermon

Happy are those whose way is made clear.
We will walk in the wisdom of God.

(Psalm 119:1)

Affirmation

**I stand in the confidence of God.
For I am convinced
that there is nothing
in death or life,
in heights or depths,
or things unseen;
there is nothing in all creation
that can separate us from the love of God.
I stand secure in the way of Christ,
in his grace and truth and love,
which is made known,
this and every day. Amen.**

(Romans 8:37-9)

(If Communion is being celebrated, continue to page 117)

Hymn

Prayer

Prayers are offered with the following response

Response

I pour out my complaint to God.
I share my trouble and my hope.

(Psalm 142:2)

Declaration

I trust I will see the goodness of God –
God's blessing for all people.
**I will wait on God, with strength and courage.
I will take heart and carry hope. Amen.**

(Psalm 27:13-14)

Hymn

Blessing

In all that is behind,
in all that lies ahead,
in every twist and turn,
may the blessing and guidance of God
keep you travelling well.
Amen.

For Reflection

What have I heard from God today?

What have I received?

How shall I live?

Let our worship continue in the unfolding of each day.

Let everyone find their voice.

Refreshment

Setting the Scene

The theme of spiritual refreshment is evident throughout the Psalms. The journey from Psalm 1 to Psalm 150 essentially speaks of the refreshment that is found in God's company, which leads to fullness of life and the continuance of praise.

Re-imagining how that refreshment is experienced and articulated today leads to an invitation in worship to dwell on everything that helps us thrive in God.

We all need at times to feel refreshed and renew our trust that God is truly making all things new. Being able to acknowledge when we are running on empty is essential if we are to keep our faith fresh and vibrant.

We find refreshment in the midst of life in so many ways – in company and in solitude, in exercise, adventure and travelling. We gather with friends and family, we find films, theatre, music and art inspirational. All this fills our lives with energy and vibrancy.

Our lives of faith should be open to the same refreshment and variety. We can encounter God again and again in new and surprising ways, when we open ourselves to that same activity and engagement.

Being refreshed by and in God, and in the company of God's people, allows us to respond to the call of the Psalmist to find our breath and voice and continue in a response of praise.

Psalm 63

When I am drained,
running on empty,
I search for you, my God.

I call to mind your love,
more sure than anything I know.
You tease a smile onto my lips,
bring a beat to my heart,
letting me breathe again.

Taking the half-full glass,
I sip slowly,
clearing my throat
to find my voice.

Secure in you,
I am moved to praise.

I cling to you, even in turmoil,
trusting I will not fall into darkness.
You have power
over all that troubles me.

I will focus more fully on you.
You sustain me now,
as you have before.

I call to mind your blessings –
you continue to set me free.

I will celebrate your love,
and find new joy in life.

With all who share this trust,
I will praise you.

For Contemplation

What is draining me this day?

Is my voice being heard?

What troubles my spirit?

Where does my focus lie?

How will I celebrate life and live with joy?

Psalm 145

I will find the words to praise you –
to call to mind
your goodness to me.
Don't ask me to understand everything fully,
but let me celebrate, just the same.

When I heard others speak of you
I only wondered –
could such a presence be for me too?
But now I know within me,
you are the Faithful One.

So let me praise you –
not worrying about using the right words,
just being honest and true.
Let my experience inspire another,
and pass on your good news.

For you are everything to me –
nothing less.
You are goodness, love and grace,
all rolled into one.

People will hear and know
and begin to understand,
when words touch hearts
and find a home.

Even if I can't make sense of it all,
you are always and for ever,
before and after,
here and now.

You open your hands
unfolding a gift.
Everyone should grab this
like an excited child!
Everything you are,
you want to share.

You answer questions not yet asked,
you fulfil promises not yet dreamed.
You are always before and behind
and watch over me.

You are close,
always here,
even now.

I will thank and bless you –
and celebrate my life in you.
I will find the words to praise you,
each day of my life.

For Contemplation

What are the blessings in my life?

How might I speak of God?

How can I inspire others to hear the good news?

What gift of God have I yet to accept?

How can I live a life of praise?

Psalm 42

With an unquenchable thirst
I long for God.
A craving consumes me,
taking over all my thoughts.

I need refreshment in life
and a new beginning.
I want God's spirit to flow,
filling me again with vibrancy.

But how do I find this?
How can God release this in me?
When I am drained I lack energy,
and my confidence seems to fade.

Do I trust God?
Do I even trust myself?

I play through my mind
times of earlier fulfilment,
when I felt I was thriving –
feeling alive in God.

So why do I forget?
Why am I sad?
Let me recover my faith and hope
and live to praise you again.

I know I can't lift myself up alone –
it's not that easy.
But God reminds me
that I have succeeded in the past,
and, with God,
can do so again.

God's presence is near;
the love of the Holy One is around me.
I find a new song rising –
a song of hope and praise.

My emotions seem to shift
from heights to depths,
from one moment to the next,
often outside my control.

I question myself, I question God,
but I will accept this
as part of who I am,
within life's ebb and flow.

God is in my longing,
in each day
and every question,
reviving me with hope and strength.

For Contemplation

What is filling my thoughts today?

What am I seeking from God?

Have I found trust in God and in myself?

When did/do I feel most alive?

Where are my emotions leading me?

What can I accept today?

Suggestions for Liturgy

Creative focus

Images that evoke refreshment could be used on screen or in a central space. Meditative music for reflection could be played in the background or used during worship for particular focus.

Hymns

As the deer pants for the water
Come, now is the time to worship
Forgiveness is your gift
In the Lord I'll be ever thankful
Longing for light, we wait in darkness
Spirit of God, come dwell within me
This is a day of new beginnings
To God be the glory, great things he hath done

Scripture readings

John 4:7–15	Jesus and the woman at the well
1 Samuel 16:1–13	David is chosen as king
John 21:15–17	Jesus restores Peter
Psalm 150	Releasing praise

Ideas to develop

Sometimes difficult encounters and questions can lead to new opportunities. Using the story of the woman at the well, explore personal encounters that have been both challenging and creative.

How might we begin to see things more as God sees them? The choosing of David as king was surprising and refreshing and led to a time of great promise. How is God seeking to surprise us today?

Stories of brokenness and restoration hold a powerful and refreshing message of the goodness of God. How does Peter's restoration by Jesus offer a message of forgiveness and hope for all?

What might be our Psalm of praise? What would it say about us and about God? What message might it hold to be shared with another generation to come?

Liturgy

Welcome

God invites us to worship as a community of faith. May you find the welcome of God here.
May our words frame a conversation with God.
Let everyone find their voice.

Invitation

Give thanks to God and bring your songs of praise.
Call on God by name, and find your voice.
God is here, and invites you in.

(Psalm 105:2)

Hymn

Call to Prayer

Search for God who is your strength.
Praise the One who is holy.
I will remember the wonders God has done.
I will lift up my voice in praise.

(Psalm 105:4-5)

Prayer

Fountain of life and love,
we praise you for every gift.
For the teeming rivers that flow with life,
for the diamond glints on surfing waves,
for the wellspring of love that never runs dry.

We worship you in the blessing of this day,
and call upon you in the watches of the night.
Awakening our senses,
you are the source of all refreshment.

We bless you in the midst of life,
with all its mystery and majesty,
for you have given us a love
that is better than anything,
in Jesus Christ your Son.

In the shadow of his transforming light,
we live and move and grow,
finding that the seeds of faith
are watered and grown.

We praise you for the Spirit's power,
to flow and fill the empty spaces
with life and joy and energy.
We are blessed to know your care.

Contemplating our reflection
in glistening pools,
we see only ourselves with regret,
and look to you with hope.
Let Christ be seen in us.

(*Silence*)

Confession (*spoken or silent*)

**Rescue me,
in every sinking feeling.
I am frozen by my fears and faults –
I cannot move.
Find me in the depths of inner darkness
and raise me to take new breath.
Revive me,
O Wellspring of Life.**

(Psalm 69:1–3)

Comforting Words

All that is frozen
is melted in the warmth of God's love.

(Psalm 147:18)

Response

**God heals our broken spirits.
How good it is to feel this love. Amen**

(Psalm 147:1, 3)

Conversation in Faith *(which may be concluded with the Lord's Prayer)*

> Our Father in heaven,
> hallowed be your name,
> your kingdom come,
> your will be done,
> on earth as in heaven.
> Give us today our daily bread.
> Forgive us our sins
> as we forgive those who sin against us.
> Save us from the time of trial
> and deliver us from evil.
> For the kingdom, the power, and the glory are yours
> now and for ever. Amen.

Hymn

The Word of God *(readings from Scripture)*

Response to the Word

Riches flow freely from God's word.
I will contemplate your wisdom.

(Psalm 119:15–16)

Hymn/Anthem/Music

Prayer before Sermon

Let peace come to those who love God's word. Amen.

(Psalm 119:165)

Sermon

Response after Sermon

Let praise be poured out from our lips.
Let me give voice to all your promises.

(Psalm 119:171-2)

Affirmation

I believe in God, the Father almighty,
>   creator of heaven and earth.

I believe in Jesus Christ, his only Son, our Lord,
>   who was conceived by the Holy Spirit
>   and born of the virgin Mary.
>   He suffered under Pontius Pilate,
>   was crucified, died, and was buried;
>   he descended to hell.
>   The third day he rose again from the dead.
>   He ascended to heaven
>   and is seated at the right hand of God the Father almighty.
>   From there he will come to judge the living and the dead.

I believe in the Holy Spirit,
>   the holy catholic church,
>   the communion of saints,
>   the forgiveness of sins,
>   the resurrection of the body,
>   and the life everlasting. Amen.

Our service continues with the celebration of Communion – turn to p. 117.

Communion Liturgy

Communion Liturgy

Invitation

Though set by human hands,
this is not our table,
but the table of Jesus Christ.

Here through Christ's presence
the ordinary is transformed.

Hymn

Story

Let us hear how this meal began.

While they were eating, Jesus took a loaf of bread, and after blessing it he broke it, gave it to the disciples, and said, 'Take, eat; this is my body.' Then he took a cup, and after giving thanks he gave it to them, saying, 'Drink from it, all of you; for this is my blood of the covenant, which is poured out for many for the forgiveness of sins.'

(Matthew 26:26–8)

Call to Prayer

Guide us to your presence,
in these holy things.
I will go the table with joy.
I will lift my heart and voice
in praise and thanksgiving.

(Psalm 43:3–4)

Prayer

We offer our love to the eternal God,
the One who is generous and faithful.
For you have brought us out of darkness
into your wonderful light.

In Jesus Christ you have brought us life,

wiping away our tears,
keeping our feet from falling.
You have shown us the way
to walk in faith,
releasing us from fear.

**What shall I offer to you,
the Great Provider?
What can I return to you?
I bring a heart broken by many regrets,
and trust in your acceptance.**

(Psalm 51:17)

**In the presence of your people
I will lift up your cup of salvation,
I will feed on the bread of life,
I will offer a sacrifice of praise,
and call upon your name.**

(Psalm 116)

Everything that is within us offers praise,
as we remember all your blessings.
You are the One who heals,
who brings new strength,
who answers prayer.

We pray for your love and grace
where only anger is known.
We pray for your generous spirit
to overcome accusation with embrace.
We pray for your open arms
to hold all people in love.

We celebrate your covenant.
We remember your commandments,
as we pray for your Holy Spirit
to bless us,
and to bless this bread and wine.

We celebrate in mystery
that in these gifts
we are lifted up with Christ,
that we might feed, in faith, on him,
to become his body in the world,
living his life, sharing his peace,
serving as he has served,
until your kingdom comes.

(Psalm 103)

**Through Jesus Christ,
the Lamb of God,
receive our prayers.
Amen.**

Communion

Gathered with his friends around a table,
Jesus shared bread and wine with his disciples.
Taking bread, blessing and breaking it, he said,
'This is my body, which is broken for you.
Do this in memory of me.'

We pray for your works of justice
for those who are oppressed.And later, taking the cup, he said,
'This cup is the new relationship with God,
made possible because of my blood.
Drink from it, all of you, to remember me.'

Response

**I will praise you.
You have answered me
and become my salvation.**

(Psalm 118:21)

Distribution

Bread and wine – these gifts of God are for you.

The Peace

May the peace of Christ be with you now and always.

(2 Thessalonians 3:16)

Let us share a sign of peace with one another.

Prayer

**It is no longer I who live,
but it is Christ who lives in me.
And the life I now live in the flesh
I live by faith in the Son of God
who loved me
and gave himself for me.**

(Galatians 2:20)

Declaration

Let everything that breathes bring praise to God.
Let everyone find their voice. Amen.

(Psalm 150:6)

Hymn

Blessing

Refreshed, nourished,
celebrating life in fullness –
may you know the blessing
of the eternal company of God,
and of all God's people,
in this and every moment.
Amen.

For Reflection

What have I heard from God today?

What have I received?

How shall I live?

Let our worship continue in the unfolding of each day.
Let everyone find their voice.

New Psalms

New Psalms

More than Words …

I do not know what to call you.
No one word expresses all I want to say.

You are God of many names,
of many people,
but I am known and loved.

I have doubted you many times.
You have known my tears and my trials,
but you are always faithful.

In anger I have wished you away,
but even as I tried to let go
you hauled me back,
making me trust again.

I wonder what you see in me
that I don't see in myself?

Why do you have faith in me
when I am called to have faith in you?

But you honour my questions and feed my thoughts.
You draw me close,
even when I want to be far away.

You have blessed me through the faith of others
who have revealed your light
even when in darkness themselves.
You have bottled up my tears with theirs,
uniting us together in you.

You are wonderfully yet mysteriously known.
I find I trust you more than anything.
You are part of me –
there is nothing without you.

Bless your people, O God, with this trust.
Let it not be a choice but a gift.

For in the midst of life
I have seen your light
and found your salvation.

I wonder at you,
I worship you,
but you are much more than all my words.

Praise be to your name.

If Today

If, for me, the sun set one last time
and I did not see it rise tomorrow,
I would still be blessed.

If I saw the stars twinkle just this night
and morning could not wake me,
I would still give you thanks.

If the whistling wind sang its tune of life
and I could listen just one last time,
I would embrace its melody.

If I could breathe in and out in continued wonder
until my last breath laboured,
I would still want to praise you.

For you, the Eternal,
called forth life,
inviting me into your company
each and every day.

Though I sometimes lost my way,
you did not hide.
When I cried out and heard no answer,
you were never absent.
The twists and turns were part of the journey,
and when I fell,
you picked me up again.

I praise you, God,
not only for your presence,
but for your people.

You have blessed me
in love and friendship,
and I count my days as happy.

You did not promise an easy path,
or life without experiencing pain.
But you give yourself eternally,
and your promises are for folk like me.

I praise you, and I pray
that others might know your care –
the healing and wholeness you bring.

Life is full when lived in you –
you are the way, the truth, the life.

I rest in you and in your peace,
now and for evermore.

Honest before God

When darkness descends
and light is hidden,
where are you, God?

When hurt and anguish
are all around,
why can't I feel you?

When life is hard
and days are long,
are you really there?

When the world seems mad
and all feels lost,
what can you actually do?

My questions are echoed
all through the ages,
by those who live in honest faith.

Faith finds a friend in doubt,
and questions are partners in learning.
Why would you mind our seeking and searching?

We do not limit you,
but only ourselves,
if we do not keep asking.

You always invite us,
ever closer, ever deeper,
to discover your wisdom.

The wise are always asking,
always seeking,
uncovering the unexpected.

Your love is surprising –
new every day.
Why doesn't it run out?

Your patience is generous,
never pushing or hurrying.
Why do you not compel us?

Your truth is a treasure,
to be gradually unfolded,
but why not make things clearer?

Listen to my questions,
O my God, and my soul.
For we wait and we wonder,
and you never tire of your people.

Which way?
What now?
Where next?
You are always asking us.

God of many questions
and answers,
keep us always
alive in you.

www.ingramcontent.com/pod-product-compliance
Lightning Source LLC
Chambersburg PA
CBHW020325010526
44107CB00054B/1982